D1247164

Greenbriar School Library
Northbrook, Illinois 60062

Amazing Mysteries

STRANGE CREATURES

John Townsend

A⁺

Smart Apple Media

Smart Apple Media
P.O. Box 3263
Mankato, MN 56002

U.S. publication copyright © 2010 Smart Apple Media. International copyright reserved in all countries.
No part of this book may be reproduced in any form without written permission from the publisher.

Printed in the United States of America

Library of Congress Cataloging-in-Publication Data

Townsend, John, 1955-
  Strange creatures / John Townsend.
      p. cm. -- (Amazing mysteries)
  Includes index.
  ISBN 978-1-59920-365-2 (hardcover)
  1. Animals, Mythical--Juvenile literature. 2. Monsters--Juvenile literature. I. Title.
  GR825.T69 2010
  398'.469--dc22
                        2008050439

Created by Q2AMedia
Editor: Honor Head
Art Director: Rahul Dhiman
Designers: Harleen Mehta, Shilpi Sarkar
Picture Researcher: Shreya Sharma
Line Artist: Sibi N. Devasia
Coloring Artists: Kusum Kala, Mahender Kumar

All words in **bold** can be found in the glossary on pages 30–31.

Picture credits
t=top b=bottom c=center l=left r=right

Cover Image: Q2AMedia, Inset: Joe Tucciarone.

Insides: Linda Bucklin/ Shutterstock: 4l, Steve Bourne: 5b, Los Angeles County Museum Of Natural History: 6, Joe Tucciarone: 9t,
Nuno Nogueira: 11b, Rene Dahinden/ TopFoto/ Fortean: 12, Rene Dahinden/ TopFoto/ Fortean: 13m, Simon: 15t, Bruce Coleman Inc./
Alamy: 19b, Bob Eggleton: 22t, Gary Simpson: 25t, Dan Varner: 26t, Robert Le Serrec/ Fortean Picture Library: 27r, Dave Watts: 28,
Royal BC Museum: 29.

Q2A Media Art Bank: 7, 8, 10, 14, 16-17, 18, 20-21, 23, 24, 31.

9 8 7 6 5 4 3 2 1

Contents

Could There Be Monsters? 4
Myths or truth—do strange creatures exist?

Creatures from the Clouds 6
Are pterosaurs and thunderbirds still flying high?

Ape-Men on the Prowl 10
Yeti, Bigfoot, and the Abominable Snowman

Secret Killers.............................. 14
Chupacabras and Death Worms—Gruesome Monsters

Mysteries of the Wild........................ 18
Giant Sloths and Prehistoric Monsters

Monsters from the Deep.................... 22
Are kraken and sea serpents lurking in the ocean depths?

The Search Continues 28
Strange creatures—not so strange now!

Glossary.................................... 30

Index and Web Finder 32

Could There Be Monsters?

Are stories of creatures hiding in forests and lurking in deep waters just myths, or could they be true?

! Dragons are creatures of myth and legend, but could people long ago have met real creatures like them?

Stories or Truth?

Myths are full of ferocious monsters that we think are just stories—but are they? Some people today swear they've seen **prehistoric** monsters and dragon-like creatures. Huge footprints have been found. People glimpse weird shadows and hear noises in the night that no one can explain.

Where Next?

Vast oceans, mountains, and deserts are some of the places where strange creatures might hide. But they could be closer than you think. People in busy cities have told of huge flying reptiles swooping through the clouds. You never know when you might come across a strange creature.

Living Dragons

People claiming to see dragons could have spotted giant lizards. The largest lizard that ever lived was the **megalania**, which could easily chase and eat a human. The bad news is, it may not be extinct. People say they've seen one in Australia. Could such creatures really be alive today?

WHAT'S THE PROOF?

- ✋ Huge footprints have been found in the Australian outback. Some experts think they could belong to megalania.
- ✋ There are reported sightings of a big monster scuttling away into the undergrowth.

EYE WITNESS

In 1979 Frank Gordon was getting into his truck in the Wattagan Mountains in New South Wales, Australia. He froze when he saw what he thought was a tree trunk moving along the ground. He stared as a giant lizard plodded away. It was about 32 feet (10 m) long or more!

❗ Could a real Megalania still be on the prowl or are the stories just far-fetched nonsense?

Creatures from the Clouds

What could be more terrifying than a screeching monster with enormous wings, knifelike talons, and a long, pointed beak swooping down from the sky to carry you away? Not possible? Read on . . .

Back from the Dead?

In 1969, a sheriff in Pennsylvania had a shock. His wife screamed at him that a huge bird was in the middle of a **creek** near their cabin. She said its wings were over 65 feet (20 m) across when it took off. The following year several people along the coast of New Jersey saw a flying creature with a "wingspread almost like an airplane."

SPOTTER'S GUIDE

Name: Thunderbird

Sighted: Parts of the USA

Features: Huge feathers, long talons, and a wingspan of more than 26 feet (8 m)

! The remains of a giant bird called a Teratorn at the Natural History Museum in Los Angeles. Could these monster birds still exist?

Return of the Thunderbird

In myths, lightning shot from the **thunderbird's** eyes and its wings made thunder when they flapped. Could this be the same creature again seen flying in Pennsylvania in 2001? A 19-year-old looked up at a noise like "flags flapping in a thunderstorm" and saw a huge bird.

The Texas Pterosaur

Two children in Texas were amazed to see a "bird" nearly 6 feet (2 m) tall standing in front of them. Jackie Davis (14) and Tracey Lawson (11) ran to get their parents. But when they returned, the creature had flown. Tracks in the mud were 8 inches (20 cm) across and showed three toes.

! A pterosaur was a huge flying reptile with wings of stretched skin.

EYE WITNESS

In 1976 three school teachers in San Antonio, Texas, saw what they described as a pterosaur swooping low over their cars. They said its wingspan was about 23 feet (7 m). It glided on huge, bony wings—like a bat's.

Attack in the Jungle

Vast swampy areas in the thick forests of Africa still hold scary secrets. Some local tribes tell of a strange flying creature that lives there called **Kongamato**, which means "breaker of boats." They say it's like a pterosaur and attacks people on rivers and lakes.

! African fishermen have told of attacks by a giant flying creature.

WHAT'S THE PROOF?

- In Zambia in 1942, Colonel Pitman found tracks with evidence of a long tail dragged over the mud.
- In 1956, an engineer saw two creatures flying slowly over a lake in Zambia. He described them as having long, thin tails and narrow heads with long, pointed snouts.

! Were the strange flying creatures seen in Africa living pterosaurs?

A Giant Vampire Bat

Two scientists crossing a river in Cameroon in 1932 came face-to-face with a huge flying creature. It had black skin and was about the size of an eagle. The men said it had pointed white teeth and "Dracula-like wings." Local people fled when they heard about it.

Is it a Bird?

Whether the Kongamato is a pterosaur or not, no one really knows. Perhaps it is a sort of large bat or bird still unknown to science. Or maybe people have really seen a shoebill stork that lives in the swampy areas of Zambia and has a wingspan of over 6.5 feet (2 m).

MYSTERY MOMENT

In 1998, Steve Romandi-Menya, a Kenyan student, said the Kongamato was still known to the bush-dwelling people in his country. The creatures are said to feed on **decomposing** human flesh by digging up bodies that aren't buried deep enough.

Ape-Men on the Prowl

In many places around the world, there are stories of huge ape-like creatures covered in hair, with arms that hang down to the ground. Are they human or animal?

SPOTTER'S GUIDE

Names: Yeti, Abominable Snowman, Bigfoot, Sasquatch

Sighted: Mountains of Asia, pine forests in Canada

Features: Over 8 feet (2.5 m) tall, long hair like an ape, disgusting smell, drags its knuckles on the ground

Footprints in the Snow

No one lives in the vast, freezing mountains in Nepal. The deep valleys and rocky caves have secrets—this is the land of the Abominable Snowman, or **Yeti**, a big, hairy monster that hides from humans. Local people call it "Yah-Teh," meaning "beast of the mountains."

! Some scientists think the Yeti may be the "missing link" between apes and humans.

10

Can You Believe It?

One story tells of a man who was lost in the mountains in 1938. He became snow blind and dazed. Before long he fell on the ice and was close to freezing to death. A nearly 10 foot (3 m) tall Yeti came out of the snow and sat by the man and gently touched him. It stayed with him until he felt well enough to continue his journey. Did this really happen or was it just a **hallucination** brought on by the man's illness?

WHAT'S THE PROOF?

- Sightings over hundreds of years
- Fuzzy photos of an ape-man
- Huge footprints in the snow
- Yaks (long-haired mountain ox) killed and their bodies left half eaten
- Tests on hair that match no known animal
- A scalp has been found, thought to be from a Yeti

Yeti Scalp

Many people have gone looking for Yetis. Some have seen footprints but not much else. There's even a Yeti Hotel in Nepal for today's tourists. Maybe a tourist will soon have a one-to-one meeting with a Yeti and get a clear photo.

Other Yeti

We may never know the truth about Yeti until someone tracks one down and gets solid proof, but in such vast and wild areas, that's a tough job. Maybe it's best to start by looking for one of Yeti's cousins. It seems ape-men roam other wild parts of the world.

! This scalp is kept in a monastery at the foot of Mount Everest. It is said to be the scalp of a Yeti.

Big Feet

The hills and forests of North America may hide a beast just like the Yeti. Native Americans have told stories for hundreds of years of "the big hairy man." Some call him **Sasquatch**—or just Bigfoot. Stories say Bigfoot knows when people go looking for him, so he hides in the mountains.

Evidence?

There have been sightings of hairy, manlike beasts in mountains and forests of North America for over 400 years, and large footprints are still found in remote areas. Every year, hundreds of reliable people report seeing strange creatures.

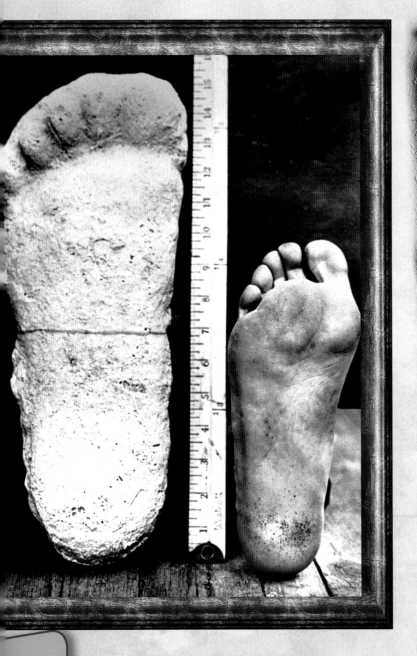

EYE WITNESS

A man reported what he saw in Arizona in 2007 as he drove to work in the morning fog. "I flipped my lights on to try and see better but it only made it worse. When I turned them off I saw a hairy man-like creature run across the road. It had to be at least 7 feet [2 m] tall. I couldn't get a good look at it because it vanished into the fog. I know for certain it wasn't a human."

! A grown man's foot beside a mold made from a mystery footprint.

Famous Film

Roger Patterson shot a famous film in 1967. He was on a horse when he came across Bigfoot and managed to film it. Some people think it's a hoax, but others think it's real. It's the only real evidence of Bigfoot anyone has ever shown.

❗ Could this be a picture of a Bigfoot running for cover in the pine forests of Canada?

© Elementary Library Mama

BATTY FOR BOOKS!

...STERY MOMENT

...d the Yowie of Australia are all
...s. Alma is said to live in the forests
...hina. Alma's fur is white up in the
...brown in the forests. In 1997,
...d giant footprints in China and
...over 441 pounds (200 kg) and at
...2 m) tall made them. Could it have
...Yeti?

Secret Killers

It is dark outside. You hear the rustle and scratch of a tree in the wind—or is it? Beware, there could be creatures on the prowl that kill in the night!

Bloodsuckers

Farmers in Mexico blame a terrifying beast for ripping apart sheep and goats in the dead of night—the **chupacabra**. They describe it as a monster, with bulging red eyes and scary fangs, about the size and shape of a baboon.

SPOTTER'S GUIDE

Name: Chupacabra (means goat-sucker)

Sighted: North and South America, Philippines

Features: 5 feet (1.5 m) tall, can leap up to 23 feet (7 m), powerful hind legs, leathery skin

❗ So far there are no clear photographs of a chupacabra. This is just one idea of how the mysterious creature might look.

! Stories of snarling beasts running through the night have been told for many years.

WHAT'S THE PROOF?

- Sheep, goats, and chickens killed in the night
- Dead animals had their blood sucked from their bodies.
- Sightings of screeching animals in the night
- Bodies of unidentifiable animals found on the roadside and near the killings
- One corpse was analyzed and declared to be a doglike reptile.

First Reports

Chupacabra attacks were first reported in American newspapers in the 1950s. Then, in 1995, several attacks in Puerto Rico hit the news. In one place alone, several hundred farm animals were killed at night. Was it just one chupacabra, or are a lot of them running wild?

Killers on the Loose

In 2008, people living in Roxas City, in the Philippines, blame the chupacabra for killing eight chickens by biting off their heads and sucking out their blood. Another farmer said his goats had puncture marks in their necks and their blood was sucked out.

Desert Terror

Another secret killer that brings terror to anyone who sees it is said to live underground in the Gobi Desert in Mongolia. The Gobi Desert covers a huge area, and very few people live there. Now and again travelers in the desert tell of their narrow escape from a strange creature that raises its deadly head above the sand. It's the Mongolian death worm.

! The death worm is said to spit yellow venom from its head. If this venom splashes on your skin, you die quickly and painfully.

SPOTTER'S GUIDE

Names: Mongolian death worm or Allghoi Khorkhoi (means cow's intestine)

Sighted: Gobi Desert

Features: 5 feet (1.5 m) long with spikes at both ends, red with dark blotches

Spitting Poison

A deadly worm? It seems absurd! Some scientists say it may be a known animal, such as a type of lizard called a skink, that burrows in the sand, but a skink isn't **venomous**. Or it could be a death adder snake that lives in sand and is related to cobras. Some cobras spit venom that is dangerous only if it gets in the eyes.

! Even fearless Mongolian warriors were said to be terrified by **Allghoi Khorkhoi.**

MYSTERY MOMENT

In 2004, an explorer named Adam Davies tried to find the Mongolian Death Worm. He met many people who swore they'd seen one, but didn't see the creature himself. "Despite our lack of success, I really believe that it's out there somewhere. The vast and remote regions in which it's said to live might explain why it's remained unknown to science. I know it's out there and I wish the next explorer the best of luck in proving me right."

Mysteries of the Wild

What better place is there for huge beasts to hide than in the thickest jungles or deepest swamps on Earth? From around the world there are stories of something nasty lurking in the wild.

At over 6.5 feet (2 m) tall, the mapinguari has long, sharp claws that can shred trees.

SPOTTER'S GUIDE

Names: Mapinguari (means defender of the forest), Brazil's Bigfoot

Sighted: Amazon rain forest

Features: Walks on two legs, over 6.5 feet (2 m) tall, hairy and reddish in color, fierce cry, foul smell, powerful claws.

Forest Fright

The Amazon rainforest is one of the largest in the world, and there may be something hiding deep inside. For more than 200 years, people in Brazil and surrounding countries have told of a huge creature that keeps well out of sight—until it needs to defend the forest. Then it attacks . . . and will kill if necessary.

Twisted Heads

Many people say they've seen a **mapinguari**. In 1975, Mário de Souza came across a giant **sloth**-like creature along the Jamauchim River in Brazil. He said, "The horrible smell hit me and made me dizzy." Some foresters swear they've seen a mapinguari kill men by twisting their heads off!

Mega Beast?

The mystery creature could be an extinct giant sloth that once roamed over all America. These giant sloths stood 6.5 feet (2 m) tall on their hind legs. Could some still be alive today?

! This model shows the size and structure of a mapinguari.

EYE WITNESS

One morning in 2003, Humberto Sosa and Susana Romano were training for a race along forest paths. They claim they heard a crashing in the bushes, then saw a strange creature like an ape, which stood over 6.5 feet (2 m) tall. It was covered in hair from head to foot. It had long arms that ended in sharp claws, an oval-shaped head, and an enormous mouth with large fangs. They kept on running!

Secret of the Swamps

The Likouala Swamp in the Congo, Africa, is one of the largest swamps in the world. It is mostly unexplored, and secrets hide deep in the middle. For more than 200 years, people living around the swamp have told of **mokele-mbembe**—the "beast that stops the rivers."

Vegetarian Killer

Local tribes are terrified of mokele-mbembe. They say it doesn't eat meat, but it will kill anyone who gets too close. They say the mokele-mbembe hates hippopotamuses and will kill them on sight, even though it doesn't eat them.

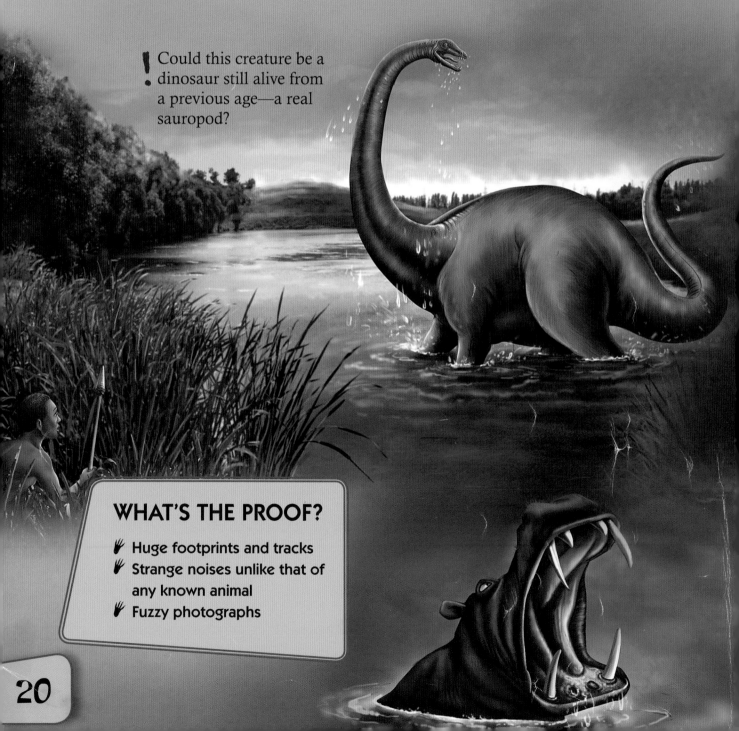

! Could this creature be a dinosaur still alive from a previous age—a real sauropod?

WHAT'S THE PROOF?

- Huge footprints and tracks
- Strange noises unlike that of any known animal
- Fuzzy photographs

Footprints and Photos

Over the years there have been many sightings of the beast. In 1992, a traveler took blurred photographs of something in Lake Tele in the Congo, that may be the head of a mokele-mbembe.

Mystery Tracks

Explorers have found footprints in mud around the swamps, with claw marks at the tips of three toes. These footprints do not belong to any known **species**. In 1932, a scientist came across huge footprints and heard strange sounds but didn't see anything.

Monsters from the Deep

Since sailors first set off across the oceans, they've told of mysterious and threatening creatures. These terrifying beasts rise up from the ocean depths to attack boats.

Sea Monsters

Reports from sailors through the ages have told of huge heads that suddenly appear above the sea to stare or to attack. Seafaring tales described strange water beasts, giant fish, horned serpents, monsters with hair, and anything in between!

Killer Kraken

In the days of sailing ships and pirates, one of the creatures most feared by sailors was the **kraken**. Stories say this sea monster with many arms could reach to the top of a ship's main mast. It could pull the ship under the waves, then eat the crew.

! Sailors dreaded what might be lurking beneath their ship.

MYSTERY MOMENT

The *Brunswick*, a Norwegian ship, was attacked three times in the 1930s by a giant squid. The creature swam close to the side of the ship and wrapped its tentacles around the **hull**. Eventually it was killed by the ship's propellers. In World War II, survivors from a sunken ship reported attacks by a giant squid. It wrapped a tentacle around one man, pulled him under the water, and ate him.

Giant Squid

Such a huge monster as the kraken was likely to be a myth, but there could well be sea creatures with tentacles almost that size. The giant squid is a real creature of great mystery. Reports have said it's over 65 feet (20 m) in length and has a beak-like mouth that can cut through steel.

! The kraken destroys a ship in the movie *Pirates of the Caribbean*. Did stories like this come from true accounts of giant squid gripping on to ships?

Sea Serpents

For hundreds of years, sailors and people on the shore have reported sea serpents slithering through the waves. Descriptions vary from a long, humped snake with a horse's or dragon's head, or a giant eel with fins, to a yellow-and-black-striped tadpole-shaped creature, or a 32-foot-(10 m) long reptile with armor.

Close Encounter

In 1848, sailors on board the ship *Daedalus* reported seeing a huge sea serpent. Captain and crew were amazed to see the enormous creature as they sailed near Cape Town, South Africa. At least 3 feet (1 m) of its head poked above the water and it seemed that there were another 65 feet (20 m) of the creature in the sea.

! Fierce and terrifying sea serpents that looked like dragons were believed to lurk beneath the water.

! Could oarfish, like this one washed up on a beach in Australia, have been mistaken for sea serpents?

Real Sea Monsters

Perhaps some sightings of sea serpents are really of long, eel-like fish called oarfish. Little is known about these animals. They live 1/2 mile (1,000 m) under the sea and only come to the surface when sick or dying. They are rarely seen alive. Some oarfish can reach over 26 feet (8 m) long.

EYE WITNESS

Captain McQuahoe of the Daedalus *said of the sea serpent, "The creature passed rapidly, but so close that had it been a man of my acquaintance I should easily have recognized his features with the naked eye." According to seven members of the crew, the serpent remained in view for around 20 minutes. Another officer wrote that the creature was more of a "lizard than a serpent."*

25

! Could the prehistoric megalodon
  still be alive today and living in
  our deepest waters?

Jaws

If you go swimming in the sea, the last
creature you'd wish to meet is a huge shark
that could swallow you whole! **Megalodon**
was a giant shark that lived millions of
years ago. It was a ferocious hunter, and
some fishermen believe it's still out there.
They've described enormous dark shadows
moving under the sea.

SPOTTER'S GUIDE

Name: Megalodon

Sighted: Deep ocean
trenches

Features: Teeth 7 inches
(18 cm) long and 1 inch
(2.5 cm) thick, body over
65 feet (20 m) long, jaws
over 6.5 feet (2 m) wide

Not Quite Extinct?

Most experts think Megalodon must be extinct. But they've been wrong before. The **coelacanth** fish suddenly showed up after scientists said it was extinct. It could be Megalodon's turn to pop up next! There were many reports by fishermen of gigantic unknown sharks—including a 98-foot (30 m) shark—at Broughton Island, Australia, in 1918.

! Does this picture, taken by Robert Le Serrec in Australia, show a monster fish, or is it a fake? No one knows for sure.

Unknown Depths

Less than five percent of the deep sea has been explored, and the deepest parts of the ocean could be a home to all sorts of amazing creatures. Deep-sea divers push back human and technological boundaries all the time to dive deeper into the ocean— and one day soon something truly fantastic will be discovered.

MYSTERY MOMENT

In 1964, Robert Le Serrec took a photo in Queensland, Australia, of a giant mystery fish. He described the monster as an enormous, dark, tadpole shape. It had a huge head and a slender, waving body that stretched to about 82 feet (25 m). He said there seemed to be a wounded area on the creature's back. But what was it?

The Search Continues

Some people would say the mysterious creatures in this book are just nonsense—from wild imaginations, dreams, or tricks. Sightings are often hard to believe because so few can ever be proven.

! Is it a bird, is it a fish? No—it's a duck-billed platypus!

Search for the Impossible

Everyone, including scientists, are fascinated by the thought that strange and rare creatures might exist, and new species are being discovered all the time. Perhaps an amazing discovery will happen very soon. Maybe some of the mysterious creatures in this book will even be proven to be real.

Hoax or Real?

When people first described an animal that was part bird, part mammal, and part fish, experts said that such a creature couldn't exist. Then someone found parts of the body of the animal. Scientists studied it and declared that a hoaxer had sewn together parts of different animals. But they were wrong —the impossible creature turned out to be the duck-billed platypus of Australia.

Mammoth Mystery

Scientists are searching in the remote forests of Thailand for hairy **mammoths**, just like the extinct woolly mammoth. People say they've seen them alive! But even if they don't find a Thai hairy mammoth, scientists aim to bring them back to life by using cells from mammoth bodies found in the ice.

Does it Exist?

A cryptid is any creature thought to exist, but which hasn't been proven. Many so-called cryptids have later been shown to be real creatures. One is the Okapi, which was once said to be a mythical creature like the unicorn. It was finally discovered in Africa in the early 1900s. The study of "hidden creatures" is called cryptozoology.

! By implanting elephants with mammoth **DNA**, scientists hope to produce a real baby mammoth by 2050.

29

Glossary

allghoi khorkhoi   the Mongolian name for the death worm

chupacabra   a blood-sucking creature of the night said to live in South America

creek   a stream or river

coelacanth   a prehistoric fish once thought to be extinct until a live one appeared in 1938

decomposing   when a dead body starts to rot away

DNA   the initials for deoxyribonucleic acid, the code inside our cells that makes each person different

extinct   when a type of animal or plant has died out so that no more exist

hallucination   what someone thinks they can see or hear something that is not really there. Can be caused by illness

hull   the bottom of a boat

kongamato   the name given to a pterosaur-like creature said to live in parts of Africa

kraken   an enormous sea monster of legend with long, powerful tentacles

legend   a story from the past based on facts that are generally accepted but cannot be proven

mammoth   large, hairy, extinct mammal of the elephant family with very long tusks that are curved upwards

mapinguari   legendary ground-dwelling, sloth-like creature with red fur living in the Amazon rainforests

megalania   fearsome giant lizard that roamed Australia and appears to have become extinct

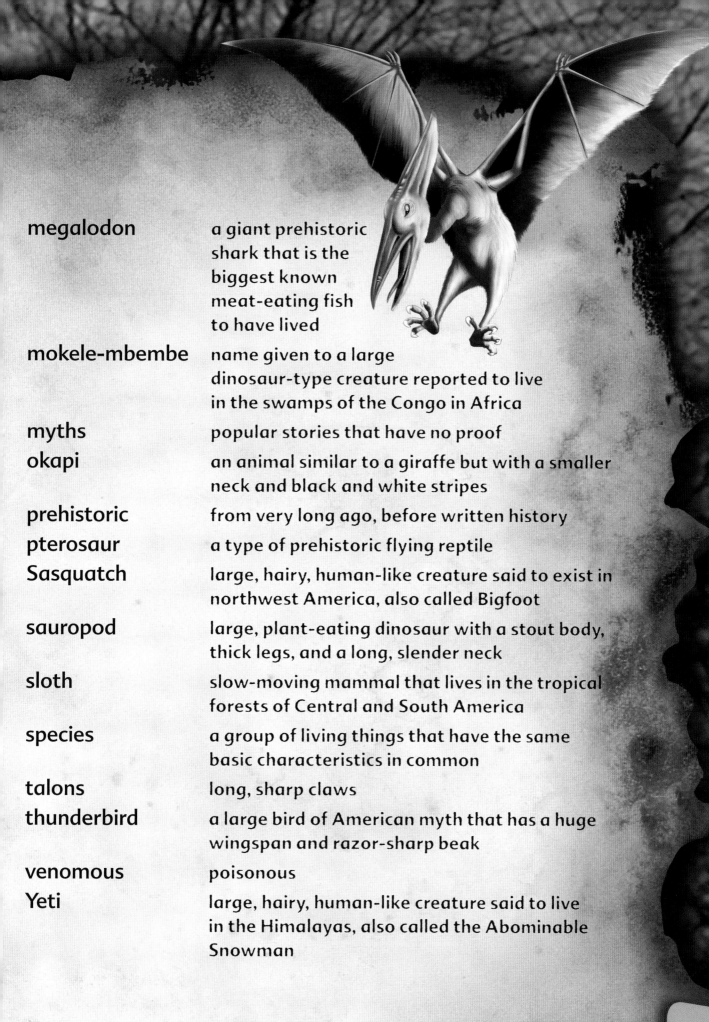

megalodon	a giant prehistoric shark that is the biggest known meat-eating fish to have lived
mokele-mbembe	name given to a large dinosaur-type creature reported to live in the swamps of the Congo in Africa
myths	popular stories that have no proof
okapi	an animal similar to a giraffe but with a smaller neck and black and white stripes
prehistoric	from very long ago, before written history
pterosaur	a type of prehistoric flying reptile
Sasquatch	large, hairy, human-like creature said to exist in northwest America, also called Bigfoot
sauropod	large, plant-eating dinosaur with a stout body, thick legs, and a long, slender neck
sloth	slow-moving mammal that lives in the tropical forests of Central and South America
species	a group of living things that have the same basic characteristics in common
talons	long, sharp claws
thunderbird	a large bird of American myth that has a huge wingspan and razor-sharp beak
venomous	poisonous
Yeti	large, hairy, human-like creature said to live in the Himalayas, also called the Abominable Snowman

Index

Abominable
    Snowman   10
allghoi khorkhoi   16,
    17
Alma   13

Bigfoot   10, 13

chupacabra   14, 15
cryptid   29
cryptozoology   29

death worm   16
dragons   4, 5

duck-billed
    platypus   28

giant squid   22

kongamato   8, 9
kraken   22, 23

mammoth   29
mapinguari   18, 19
megalodon   26, 27
megalonia   5
mokele-mbembe   20

oarfish   25

pterosaur   7, 8, 9

Sasquatch   10, 12
sea serpent   24, 25
skink   17

thunderbird   6

Yeti   10, 11, 12
Yowie   13

Web Finder

http://www.unmuseum.org/unmain.htm
Museum of Unnatural History

http://www.unmuseum.org/bigfoot.htm
Reveals evidence of Bigfoot sightings across North America

http://www.strangemag.com
Magazine articles that explore strange phenomena

http://www.newanimal.org/
A list of articles about the strange creatures that make up cryptozoology!